Mockingbird
Noisy Mimic

by Natalie Lunis

Consultant: Robin W. Doughty
Professor Emeritus
Department of Geography and the Environment
The University of Texas at Austin
Author of *The Mockingbird*

BEARPORT PUBLISHING

NEW YORK, NEW YORK

Credits

Cover and Title Page, © Chesapeake Images/Shutterstock and © Johann Schumacher; TOC, © Chesapeake Images/Shutterstock; 4–5, © Exactostock/SuperStock; 6, © Lee F. Snyder/Photo Researchers, Inc.; 7T, © Chris Lorenz/Dreamstime; 8, © All Canada Photos/SuperStock; 9, © Cathy Hennessy/Distinctive Images/Flickr/Getty Images; 10–11, © Lauri Ward; 12L, © Barbara Mowery/Flickr/Getty Images; 12R, © Ken Slade; 13, © Larry Ditto/BCI/Photoshot; 14T, © Jay Paredes/Beauty of the Wild; 14B, © Toni Ard/Flickr/Getty Images; 15, © Lou Guillette/WENN/Newscom; 16, © Rolf Nussbaumer/Nature Picture Library; 17, © William Leaman/The Image FInders; 18, © Ezekiel Phillips; 19, © Diana Russler and Bill Gent/Allegria Photos; 20, © Laura Riley/BCI/Photoshot; 21, © FLPA/S & D & K Maslow/age fotostock; 22, © Julie M. Nace; 23TL, © Lee F. Snyder/Photo Researchers, Inc.; 23TM, © Kenneth H. Thomas/Photo Researchers, Inc.; 23TR, © Cathy Hennessy/Distinctive Images/Flickr/Getty Images; 23BL, © Perica Dzeko/Shutterstock; 23BR, © Toni Ard/Flickr/Getty Images; 24, © Gerald A. DeBoer/Shutterstock.

Publisher: Kenn Goin
Editorial Director: Adam Siegel
Creative Director: Spencer Brinker
Cover Design: Dawn Beard Creative and Kim Jones
Photo Researcher: Picture Perfect Professionals, LLC

Library of Congress Cataloging-in-Publication Data

Lunis, Natalie.
  Mockingbird : noisy mimic / by Natalie Lunis.
     p. cm. — (Animal loudmouths)
  Includes bibliographical references and index.
  ISBN-13: 978-1-61772-277-6 (library binding)
  ISBN-10: 1-61772-277-4 (library binding)
  1. Mockingbirds—Juvenile literature. I. Title.
  QL696.P25L86 2012
  598.8'44—dc22
                              2011007785

For more information, write to Bearport Publishing Company, Inc., 45 West 21st Street, Suite 3B, New York, New York 10010. Printed in the United States of America in North Mankato, Minnesota.

073011
042711CGE

10 9 8 7 6 5 4 3 2 1

Contents

Singing in Spring 4

A Double Message 6

The Perfect Home 8

Finding a Mate 10

Building a Nest 12

Defending the Nest 14

Baby Birds 16

Growing Up Fast 18

Listening and Learning 20

Sound Check 22

Glossary 23

Index 24

Read More 24

Learn More Online 24

About the Author 24

Singing in Spring

Early on a spring morning, a mockingbird sits high up on a tree branch.

It lifts its head, opens its beak, and starts to sing loudly.

Unlike other birds, however, it does not sing just one kind of song.

It can mimic, or copy, the songs of more than 30 other birds.

It can even mimic the sounds of barking dogs, chirping crickets, and car alarms.

The mockingbird's name comes from its special talent. At one time, *mock* meant the same thing as "to mimic."

A Double Message

The noisy singer on the tree branch is a male mockingbird.

The little gray bird keeps on singing as he flies from the tree branch to a rooftop to the top of a telephone pole.

These spots mark the outer edges of the mockingbird's **territory**.

The male's loud, long-lasting song warns other males to stay out of this area.

At the same time, it tells females that he is ready to attract a **mate** and start a family there.

When a male mockingbird is looking for a mate in the spring or summer, he often sings all day. Sometimes he sings all night, too.

The Perfect Home

Mockingbirds live in some parts of Canada and Mexico, and in most parts of the United States.

Most often, they live near people.

Their favorite homes are backyards and parks that have grassy areas, as well as trees and **shrubs**.

Mockingbirds in the Wild

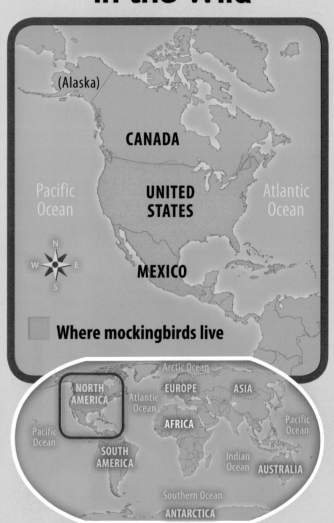

(Alaska)

CANADA

Pacific Ocean

UNITED STATES

Atlantic Ocean

MEXICO

N W E S

Where mockingbirds live

Arctic Ocean

NORTH AMERICA

Atlantic Ocean

EUROPE

ASIA

Pacific Ocean

AFRICA

Pacific Ocean

SOUTH AMERICA

Indian Ocean

AUSTRALIA

Southern Ocean

ANTARCTICA

The mockingbird is the state bird of five U.S. states: Arkansas, Florida, Mississippi, Tennessee, and Texas.

9

Finding a Mate

When a female mockingbird hears a male singing day after day, she knows that he will be a good mate.

His loud, strong voice tells her that he has found a good area for building a nest.

It also tells her that he is ready to defend his territory against other males.

The female does not **communicate** with the male by singing back, however.

Instead, two mockingbirds that have paired up check in with each other by making soft, short *hew-hew* sounds.

Female mockingbirds are able to sing their own songs and imitate other birds. However, they do so during the fall and winter when they spend time on their own.

Building a Nest

Once two mockingbirds become mates, they start to build a nest together in a tree or shrub.

The male uses twigs to make a cup-shaped outer layer.

The female uses pieces of grass and leaves to make a soft inner layer.

Then she lays from three to six small eggs inside the nest.

twig for building a nest

eggs in a nest

adult mockingbird in a nest

Mockingbirds usually build their nest from three to ten feet (1 to 3 m) off the ground—lower than the nests of many other kinds of birds.

Defending the Nest

Both male and female mockingbirds fiercely defend their nest.

They chase away owls, crows, and hawks through the air.

All these large birds hunt for eggs and baby birds to eat.

The mockingbirds also swoop down and attack cats, snakes, squirrels, and any other animal that might try to sneak into the nest from below.

mockingbird

crow

Often mockingbirds attack more than just the enemies that eat their eggs or babies. They also go after people and dogs that get too close to their nests.

Baby Birds

The eggs in a mockingbird's nest **hatch** about 12 days after they are laid.

At first the babies cannot see and are unable to fly.

Their parents take turns finding insects and berries for them to eat.

When the adult comes back with the food, the baby birds make peeping sounds and open their mouths wide.

Then the parent drops the food in.

parent feeding babies

During the night, a mother mockingbird stays in the nest with her babies to keep them warm.

17

Growing Up Fast

Baby mockingbirds grow up fast.

About 12 days after hatching, they are able to see and fly.

They are still not ready to live on their own, however.

For about another three weeks, they still need to be fed by their parents.

All day long, they follow the adults around and make peeping sounds to ask for food.

young mockingbird

In warmer places, a pair of mockingbirds may raise up to four sets of babies each spring and summer. As soon as one set of eggs hatches, the male starts building a new nest.

parent feeding young mockingbird

Listening and Learning

As a mockingbird grows up, it listens and learns.

The songs that come from the adults around it become its first songs.

Then, when it is older and finds a territory of its own, it keeps on learning new songs and new sounds.

For the rest of its life, the little gray bird keeps listening and singing, filling the air with the songs of many different birds.

white patch

white patch

An adult mockingbird is 9 to 11 inches (23 to 28 cm) long, including its long tail. When it flies, it shows two large white patches that are on the underside of its wings.

Sound Check

Mockingbirds can use their voices in two different ways. They can sing songs, and they can make short sounds known as calls.

Songs

Songs are made up of groups of sounds that form patterns. Like other songbirds, mockingbirds sing mainly for two reasons—to attract mates and to tell other birds that they are ready to protect their territories.

Calls

Calls are much shorter than songs. They are usually made up of a single sound or just a few sounds. Like the calls of other birds, mockingbird calls have specific uses and meanings. Here are the most important ones:

Call	Used for
a soft *hew-hew*	checking in with a mate
a harsh *hew-hew*	chasing enemies or other mockingbirds away
chak	warning sound that enemies are in the nest area

Glossary

communicate (kuh-MYOO-nuh-kayt) to pass on information, ideas, or feelings

hatch (HACH) to reach the point when an animal comes out of an egg

mate (MAYT) one of a pair of animals that have young together

shrubs (SHRUBZ) plants that have many woody stems

territory (TER-uh-*tor*-ee) an area of land that belongs to and is defended by an animal or a group of animals

23

Index

babies 14–15, 16–17, 18–19

calls 22

eggs 12, 14–15, 16, 19

enemies 14–15, 22

females 6, 10, 12, 14

food 16, 18–19

homes 8

males 6–7, 10, 12, 14, 19

mates 6–7, 10, 12, 22

nest 10, 12–13, 14–15, 16–17, 19, 22

singing 4, 6–7, 10, 20, 22

size 21

state bird 9

territory 6, 10, 20, 22

Read More

Burton, Philip. *Spotter's Guide to Birds of North America.* Tulsa, OK: EDC Publishing/Usborne (1991).

Harrison, George H. *Backyard Bird Watching for Kids.* Minocqua, WI: Willow Creek Press (1997).

Landau, Elaine. *State Birds.* New York: Franklin Watts (1992).

Learn More Online

To learn more about mockingbirds, visit
www.bearportpublishing.com/AnimalLoudmouths

About the Author

Natalie Lunis has written many science and nature books for children. She lives in the Hudson River Valley, just north of New York City.